GW00647727

HASTINGS

Beautiful Town

HASTINGS
Beautiful Town

Oliver Tookey

breedon **books**
PUBLISHING

First published in Great Britain in 2009 by
The Breedon Books Publishing Company Limited
Breedon House, 3 The Parker Centre,
Derby, DE21 4SZ.

© Oliver Tookey, 2009

All Rights Reserved. No part of this publication may be
reproduced, stored in a retrieval system, or transmitted
in any form, or by any means, electronic, mechanical,
photocopying, recording or otherwise without the prior
permission in writing of the copyright holders, nor be
otherwise circulated in any form or binding or cover
other than in which it is published and without a similar
condition being imposed on the subsequent publisher.

A catalogue record for this book is available from the
British Library.

ISBN 978-1-85983-703-0

Printed and bound by MKT Print, Slovenia.

CONTENTS

DEDICATION

This book is dedicated to the good people of Hastings.

INTRODUCTION

Located in East Sussex, directly on the English Channel, Hastings is one of the most historical towns in Great Britain. It is famous for the Battle of Hastings in 1066; however, as visitors to the town have found, Hastings has much more to it than this. It has a unique charm and character all of its own, and has attracted people from all over the world. Its cosmopolitan culture is full of welcome surprises, yet the traditional British seaside culture is still alive and well. Neighbouring Hastings is St Leonards-on-Sea, and the two towns are often regarded as being one and the same. However, St Leonards has its own character too, and some breathtaking architecture.

In recent years the town's economy has steadily improved, largely due to government funding and the pool of creative talent within the town. The phrase 'Hastings is on the up' is often heard, and many exciting projects are in development.

Surrounding Hastings is some of the most stunning scenery in the South East. The country park begins at the east of the town and offers some breathtaking walks along the cliff top. To the west, in St Leonards, is the little-known Filsham Reed Bed nature reserve, which attracts water foul all year round and is partially flooded during the winter months.

Like many seaside towns, Hastings has its own pier. Unfortunately, years of storms and limited funding have left it in need of repair, and most of it is closed to the public for safety reasons. However, there is a concerted effort being made to re-open the pier, and it is unlikely it will be left to fall into the sea.

Perhaps the most striking thing about the town is the unique mix of people who live here, and who will surely keep Hastings on the map for years to come.

HASTINGS CASTLE

Hastings Castle is situated on the West Hill, overlooking the town centre. Construction of a timber and earth fort began in 1066 on the instruction of William the Conqueror shortly before the Battle of Hastings. In 1070 William gave orders for the original castle to be rebuilt in stone, and in 1220 Henry III strengthened the castle, but in 1287 violent storms resulted in much of it collapsing into the sea.

Throughout the centuries the castle further succumbed to the elements, and in the 16th century, during Henry VIII's Dissolution of the Monasteries, the castle was ransacked of its valuables and left open to further erosion. The castle became so overgrown that it was not rediscovered and excavated until 1824. During this period Hastings was one of the more popular Victorian resorts and the castle became a tourist attraction.

The castle was further damaged during bombing raids in World War Two, and in 1951 the Hastings Corporation purchased the castle and turned it into the tourist attraction that it is to this day.

The west side of the castle.

Hastings Castle, overlooking the pier. The archway was part of the Chapel of the Holy Cross, while the tower is the remains of the chapel's entrance or nave. The southern section of the castle and the keep eroded into the sea during the 13th century.

The remains of the chapel's nave.

The chapel archway
Part of the arch was
rebuilt after excavation
in 1824.

The outline of the chapel can still be seen.

Dungeons

The dungeons at Hastings Castle are known as the 'Whispering Dungeons'. They have been given this name because even the slightest sound at one end can be heard clearly at the other. It has been suggested that the dungeons were designed with these acoustics to help interrogators eavesdrop on their prisoners' secrets.

Castle wall
Originally a pre–fabricated wooden fort, the castle was rebuilt from stone in 1070 under orders issued by William the Conqueror.

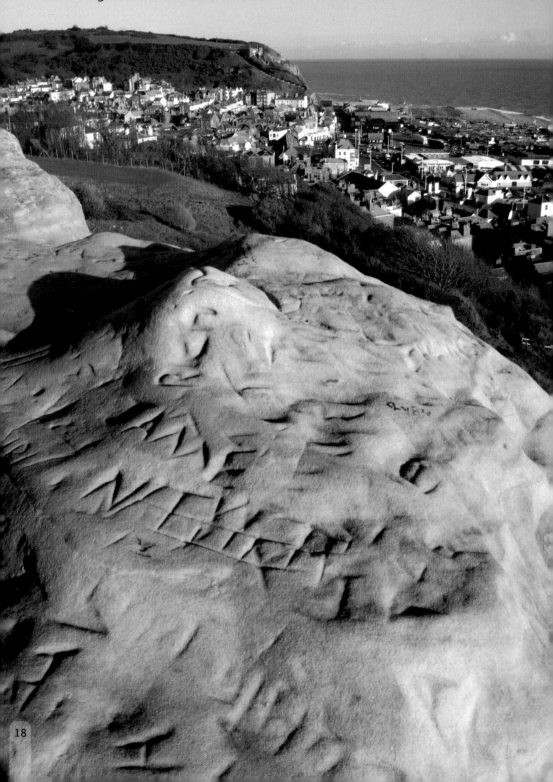

The soft sandstone of the West Hill has been eroded over the years, resulting in unusual formations.

The soft sandstone of the West Hill makes it a popular place to engrave names.

A view from 'Ladies Parlour' adjacent to the castle. The remains of an Iron Age fort have been discovered on this site.

ST MARY IN THE CASTLE

The Church of St Mary in the Castle was built in 1828 by Joseph Kay for the Earl of Chichester, after the castle cliffs had been cut away. It became derelict in the 1970s until it was rescued by the Friends of St Mary in the Castle and turned into an art centre in 1997. Inside is a 500-seat circular auditorium and theatre.

Pelham Crescent.

The Regency-style houses of Pelham Crescent.

The Georgian Church of St Mary in the Castle forms the centrepiece of Pelham Crescent.

ST CLEMENTS CAVES

St Clements Caves are a labyrinth of caves that lie under the West Hill. They were formed through natural erosion of the sandstone rock and have since been expanded upon through excavation. The first written record of the caves dates from 1786 when a married couple described living there after being evicted from their home.

Two hundred years ago the caves were used to hide contraband smuggled in by local gangs. However, it has been suggested that the smugglers could have easily been caught as there are a limited number of escape routes.

During the war they were used as an air-raid shelter, harbouring some 500 people at a time, and in the 1960s they became a popular venue for bands. Now called The Smugglers Adventure, the caves are themed around smuggling exploits of the 18th century. Visitors can interact with video and audio exhibits, as well as witness full-size wax figures of smugglers fighting the law.

An engraving found in the caves.

'Monks Walk' – a 140ft–long tunnel marks the entrance to the caves.

Large caverns lie within the cave system.

A recreation of conflict between a smuggler and the law.

The labyrinth of caves can be found under the West Hill.

Adjacent to the caves is this old look-out post.

THE BATTLE OF HASTINGS

The Battle of Hastings took place on 14 October 1066 between the Norman army of William the Conqueror and the Saxon army led by Harold Godwinson, King Harold II. It was the last time a foreign power successfully invaded the British Isles.

The battle itself took place on Senlac Hill in the present town of Battle, approximately six miles north west of Hastings. The Norman had an army of 8,400, consisting of 2,200 cavalry, 4,500 infantry and 1,700 archers. The Saxon army numbered 7,500 and was entirely made up of infantry. During the battle the Normans weakened the Saxons with an initial arrow attack, followed by attacking waves of cavalry and infantry. The main battle lasted just one day and it is estimated that 5,000 Saxons and 3,000 Norman were killed. Tradition states that King Harold II was killed by an arrow in the eye, although this has never been proven.

After the battle William rested his army in Hastings for two weeks before advancing to London with re-enforcements. Edgar the Atheling, who was crowned king after Harold's death, along with Esegar the Sheriff of London and two northern earls, submitted to William. The Norman duke was crowned king of England on Christmas Day 1066 at Westminster Abbey.

The legacy of the Norman victory had a profound effect on British history. Perhaps the most influential was the introduction of old French words into the English language by the ruling classes. Another change was the government: before the Norman victory England was governed by many autonomous administrations known as 'shires' which were run by sheriffs (from shire reeve).

The Norman centralised this system and in 1086 the *Domesday Book* recorded who held what property and what taxes they were liable for.

Norman soldiers preparing for battle.

Battle Abbey, built by William the Conqueror to commemorate those who died.

The Saxon army preparing for battle.

The Battle of Hastings re-enactment takes place every year on Senlac Hill.

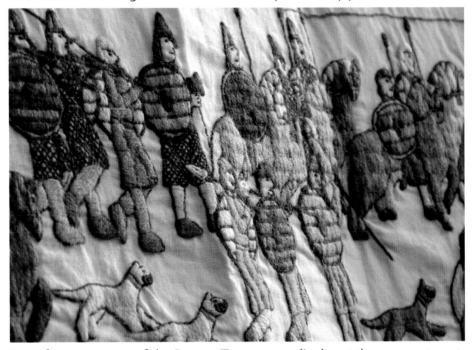

Part of a woven copy of the Bayeux Tapestry on display at the re-enactment.

An archer demonstrating his skills
at the re-enactment.

Woodland surrounds the battle site.

THE TOWN CENTRE

Hastings town centre was built in the 19th century and surrounds the site of the old clock tower – known as the Albert Memorial – which stood until the 1970s. Although no trace of it remains today, the area is still known as the memorial.

One of the biggest attractions is the Priory Meadow Shopping Centre. It was built on the site of the Priory Meadow Cricket Ground, which hosted County Cricket until 1989 and some well-known cricketers played there.

Just to the west of the town centre lies the Claremont area, or 'America ground'. A vast shingle bank had built up in the area and people quickly realised that no one owned the land, and so began to live there rent free. By the 1820s a community of over 1,000 lived and worked there, and the new and fashionable resort of Hastings requested that the government remove these 'beggars, gypsies and other undesirables'. The community responded by claiming they were independent of Hastings and raised the American flag in defiance.

The north side of the town centre.

Traditional fish 'n' chip shops are found throughout the town.

The castle on the West Hill overlooks the town.

Statue of a cricketer commemorating the county cricket ground, now the Priory Meadow Shopping Centre.

A view from inside Queens Arcade.

Holy Trinity Church on Robertson Street.

The seafront side of Hastings town centre.
Robertson Street can be seen leading into the town.

The town hall was designed by Henry Ward, a prolific architect who was
responsible for many buildings in the Hastings area. It was built in 1880.

Hastings station is within walking distance of the town centre. It was originally constructed in 1851 and was reconstructed in a neo-Georgian style in 1931. In 2004 the station was again rebuilt in a modernist style. It connects Hastings to Eastbourne and Brighton to the west, London to the north, and Ashford International and the Channel Tunnel to the east.

Hastings train station.

Wellington Square, a large green space in the town centre.

The entrance to Hastings library and information centre.

The back of the library and information centre.

The town centre underpass connects the new town to the old.

A mural in the underpass depicting the Battle of Hastings.

Hastings Museum and Art Gallery, a few minutes walk from the town centre.

Used with permission of Hastings Museum and Art Gallery.

Used with permission of Hastings Museum and Art Gallery.

The magnificent Durbar Hall in the Hastings Museum. It was designed for the Indian and Colonial Exhibition of 1886.

Hastings Mayoress Maureen Charlesworth (centre) at the annual town crier competition.

THE PIER AND SEAFRONT

Hastings Pier was opened on the first ever Bank Holiday – 5 August 1872 – by Lord Warden of the Cinque Ports Earl of Granville.

The pier has gone through several changes throughout its existence: its original 2,000-seat pavilion was destroyed by fire in 1917, and a less elaborate structure rebuilt in 1922. In the 1960s top acts such as Pink Floyd, The Rolling Stones and Jimi Hendrix graced its stage. During the 1980s its disco and arcade became popular with teenagers, and during the 1990s many art and craft shops opened. However, during recent years the pier has experienced a decline in popularity, and failed to receive millennium funding in 1996.

Today, most of the pier is closed to the public, except for the area nearest the promenade. This is due to structural damage from the relenting action of the sea and frequent storms.

Despite the damage, efforts are being made to re-open the pier and put this landmark back on the map.

The countless storms over the years have left
the end section of the pier unsafe and it is
currently closed to the public.

The pier is perhaps the best-known landmark in Hastings.

The seaward side of the pier is still open to the public and plans are underway to open the rest of it up again.

A view of the pier.

Shops on the pier have been forced to close because of damage to the structure.

Morris dancers on the pier as part of the Jack-in-the-Green Festival.

Crowds gather to watch Morris dancers on the pier. The White Rock Theatre can be seen in the background.

Near to the pier are the Palace Bars.

Hastings Pier.

The seafront at night.

Coiled sand castings are created by lugworms under the sand.

Fishermen collect lugworms from the sands at low tide and use them for bait.

During the summer the beach becomes crowded with tourists and locals.

The beach near the pier at low tide with Marine Court in the background.

ST LEONARDS

St Leonards-on-Sea is part of Hastings and lies west of the town as far as Bexhill. Its origins date back to the early 19th century, when it was built for the well-off, who liked to spend their holidays on the coast. Since then it has extended well beyond its original boundaries, but old St Leonards can still be found.

The famous architect James Burton, who designed houses in London's Bloomsbury and Regent's Park, was responsible for many buildings in St Leonards, some of which still exist today. These include houses around St Leonards Gardens, his own home on the seafront and houses in Mercatoria, originally a shopping area. His most prominent building in the area is the Royal Victoria Hotel on St Leonards seafront.

After his death in 1837, his son Decimus Burton (1800–81) took over and extended the area of the new town. He built houses around Maze Hill and a school, which is now part of Hastings College.

During this time a rail link from London reached the town and Warrior Square Station opened in 1852. A pier was built opposite the Royal Victoria Hotel in 1891 but was cut in half during World War Two to protect against invasion. The remainder was finally destroyed in 1951.

Any visitor to St Leonards will undoubtedly notice Marine Court, the large Art-Deco building on the seafront that resembles an ocean liner. It was built in 1937 and at the time was the tallest block of flats in the country. The architects, K. Dalgleish and R.K. Pullen, were part of the Modern Movement, which aimed to improve peoples quality of life through architecture. Although not to everyone's liking, the building was listed in 1999. Today it is illuminated by blue lights.

Leisure boats from the Hastings yacht club on St Leonards beach.

The statue of Queen Victoria in front of Warrior Square Gardens.

The beach opposite Warrior Square Gardens during low tide. The rock formation is known as 'goat ledge'.

James Burton's Assembly Rooms, now know as the Masonic Hall.

Burton's South Lodge has a double villa design and serves as the entrance to St Leonards Gardens.

Crown House on St Leonards seafront was James Burton's purpose-built residence and the first house to be built in St Leonards.

Legend has it that William the Conqueror dined on this rock after landing at Bulverhythe.

A contemporary bar and restaurant on St Leonards promenade.

The Royal Victoria Hotel, Burton's centrepiece for St Leonards, was opened in 1828. Past guests include Queen Victoria, King George V, Prince Albert and Edward VII.

THE ROY

Best Western
ROYAL VICTORIA HOTEL

Burton's North Lodge, or 'Haggard House', previously a toll gate.

A plaque outside the house of Sir Henry Rider Haggard. The famous
adventure novelist lived here between 1918 and 1923.

THIS STONE
ERECTED AD 1828
MARKS THE EASTERN
BOUNDARY AT THIS
POINT OF THE TOWN
OF ST LEONARDS
FOUNDED BY THE LATE
JAMES BURTON ESQ
1828

This is all that remains of St Leonards Archway. It was built in 1828 and marked the boundary between the two towns. It was secretly knocked down overnight in 1859 by the council, which shocked the locals.

St Leonards Parish Church was originally built in a Gothic style by James Burton in 1833 . However, it was destroyed in the war by a doodlebug. The church was rebuilt and opened again in 1955.

The Clock Tower overlooks St Leonards Gardens. The Gothic–style tower was once used as the official timekeeping piece for St Leonards. The clock was made by George III's clockmaker.

St Johns Church on Pevensey Road is the fourth church to have been built on the site in the last 150 years.

St Leonards Warrior Square Station, opened in 1852.

Marine Court on St Leonards seafront. At the time of its construction it was the largest block of flats in the country. The Art-Deco building resembles a passenger liner.

The pyramid-shaped
Burton family tomb,
situated near Hastings
College, West Hill Road,
St Leonards.

Engravings on the Burton family tomb on West Hill Road.

St Leonards promenade during a fairly uncommon snow flurry.

THE WRECK OF THE *AMSTERDAM*

Found in the sands of Bulverhythe is the wreck of the *Amsterdam*. When the tide is low enough the ship's outline can be seen protruding through the sand, while beneath the sand three decks lie largely preserved. The Dutch East Indiaman ran aground during a severe storm on 26 January 1749. It is said that the crew were suffering from the plague and mutinied on the ship's maiden voyage to Java.

Local smugglers soon raided the ship of its silver bullion. Word got around and people began fighting one another, which resulted in a man being shot on the beach.

The *Amsterdam* is of archaeological importance as she is the most complete East Indiaman wreck in the world. In the 1980s archaeological excavations were carried out by British and Dutch teams.

Near to the *Amsterdam* are the remains of a petrified forest.

The wreck of the *Amsterdam* can be spotted at low tide.

At low tide it is possible to walk along the sands from Bulverhythe towards the town.

The remains of a 6,500-year-old petrified forest
can be seen protruding through the sand.

These colourful beach huts line the beach close to the *Amsterdam* wreck.

Local shrimp fisherman walking along the beach at Bulverhythe.

Sea defences have been built along the beach at Bulverhythe to absorb the energy of the waves and protect the adjacent railtrack.

THE OLD TOWN

The Old Town is the original Hastings town and some of its buildings can be traced back to the 15th century. It lies in the Bourne Valley, between the East and West Hills, and a river called the Bourne once ran through the town but now runs underground.

A view across the Old Town from the East Hill steps.

Some of the houses date from the 15th century.

Hastings Old Town and pier at night.

There are many historical plaques dotted around the town. Apparently nothing happened here though!

Artist Barbara Leigh Smith was one of the founders of the women's rights movement. She studied politics and law, and her publications helped change the law on women's right to vote. She frequently stayed at the family home on Pelham Crescent.

Catherine Cookson lived in Hastings between 1930 and 1976. She originally worked as the manager at the Hastings laundry workhouse, and began her first novel in the town in 1946. Her books went on to sell over 120 million copies.

The Seagate erected at the foot of the High Street was part of the town wall, which was built along the mouth of the River Bourne.

The Old Town Chess
Square on George Street.

The oldest house in Hastings
stands at number 31 The Bourne.
It dates from 1450 and was once
a courthouse.

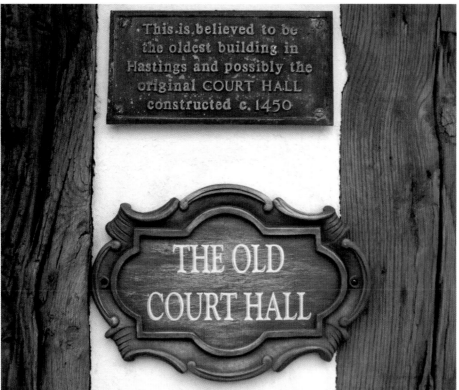

A plaque outside the oldest house in Hastings.

A hanging basket on an Old Town Tudor house.

Many of the houses still retain their original features.

The Old Town Museum on the High Street.

The 15th-century Tudor houses along All Saints Street.

Passageways can be found throughout the Old Town.

St Clements Church.

GEORGE STREET

George Street marks the beginning of the Old Town and leads from the West Hill Lift entrance to the High Street. Rows of shops, houses and pubs line the street on both sides. Some of the more popular pubs include the trendy Dragon Bar, which regularly exhibits work by local artists, and the Hastings Arms, a favourite haunt of local musicians.

Shops, restaurants and pubs line the pedestrianised George Street.

A variety of rooftops along George Street.

WHITE'S
SEAFOOD
&
STEAK
BAR

Legend states that this public house is not in fact Tudor but dates from 1946; however, other sources claim it is much older.

SHEPHERD NEAME

YE OLDE PUMPHOUSE

YE OLDE PUMPHOUSE

Smugglers Bar

THURS PIANO NIGHT

Ye Olde Pump House

The Daily Telegraph

for Gastro Pub Food

Now Inside

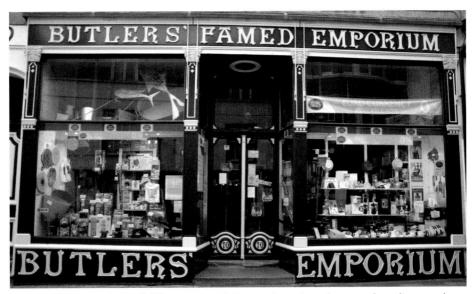

Originally called Penfolds, Butlers' Emporium has been a hardware shop since 1836.

The West Hill Lift welcomes the visitor to George Street. This underground lift leads up to the West Hill.

George Street House, where watercolourist Samuel Prout, famous for his architectural drawings, lived from 1837 to 1844.

THE HIGH STREET

The High Street is one of the oldest streets in the Old Town and was originally named Market Street. It runs from the east of George Street uphill towards Old London Road. Like George Street, it has a mix of shops, pubs and houses, as well as the Old Town Museum and the Electric Palace independent cinema. Some of the Tudor houses date back to the 15th century and their age can clearly be seen in their distorted shapes and woodworm–holed timber. The High Street is also home to the garden of remembrance. This was originally the Swan Inn, which dated back to the 16th century; however, it was destroyed by an air raid in 1943.

Left: Smoked brickwork can be seen on this building on the High Street.

Below: The memorial marking the site of the Swan Inn. The building was in constant use from the 1523 until it was bombed during World War Two in May 1943. It was once the posting house for coaches from Brighton, Dover and London.

One of the many antique and junk shops along the High Street.

The High Street has the highest percentage of listed buildings in the town.

The Mews, just off the High Street, is a collection of antique and junk shops.

This propeller was trawled from the sea by local fisherman Richard Ball. It is believed to be from a German Heinkel Bomber aircraft. The site where it stands was bombed during World War Two on 23 May 1943.

ALL SAINTS STREET

Together with the High Street, All Saints Street is one of the oldest streets in Hastings. It does not have the retail outlets like George Street and the High Street, but it is home to some of the oldest buildings in the town, including Shovell House, the residence of Admiral Sir Cloudsley Shovell's family (pictured right).

The Cinque Ports pub on All Saints Street.

123

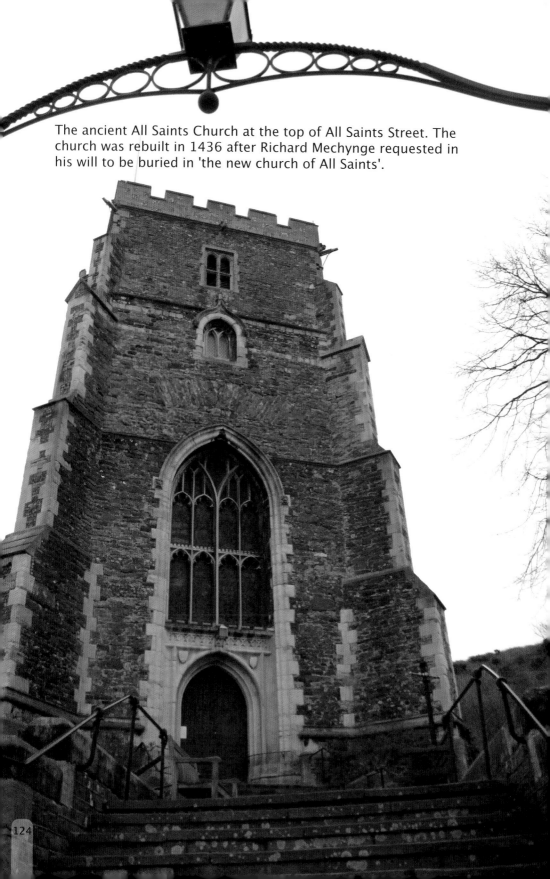

The ancient All Saints Church at the top of All Saints Street. The church was rebuilt in 1436 after Richard Mechynge requested in his will to be buried in 'the new church of All Saints'.

Just off All Saints Street, the Piece of Cheese Cottage is the only three-sided cottage in England and the second smallest. It was built in 1871 for a £5 bet.

THE STADE

The Stade fishing area dates back at least 1,000 years. It runs from Winkle Island junction and stretches as far as Rock-a-Nore beach. The word Stade is of Saxon origin, meaning 'landing place', and originates from the Battle of Hastings.

In 1887 a groyne was erected at the east of Rock-a-Nore. In 1896 much of the current harbour arm was built, although previous harbours have been there since the 1500s and remains can be found under the boating lake.

The build up of shingle between the harbour and the groyne resulted in the beach expanding seawards, resulting in more room for the fishing fleet. Today the Stade is home to Europe's largest beach-launched fishing fleet and is one of the few remaining in the country. Each vessel has its own engine and winch, which was traditionally operated by a 'boy ashore', and tractors push the boats into the sea. The launching of boats in this manner restricts their size, kit and range, thus limiting the ecological damage they have on local fisheries. The RX registration on the boats means they are part of the Rye and Hastings fleet.

A unique feature which has attracted many tourists and painters to Hastings are the tall net shops or deezes. They are made from timber coated with black tar and are used to store fishing nets and keep them dry. Their tall construction maximises space on limited plots, thereby saving the fishermen money. However, today's nets are often left on the beach as the material they are made from does not rot easily.

Historically, the fishermen lived in the All Saints and St Clements areas of the Old Town. Many still live and drink there and have a tough reputation.

The Hastings Lifeboat Station. The town has two lifeboats and they are called out an average of 50 times a year.

The Old Town boating lake and funfair.
The lake was built over the original
Elizabethan harbour.

The harbour arm provides an excellent
view of the fishing fleet and East Hill.

The Fishermen's Museum on Rock-a-Nore Road, where you can find a full-size traditional fishing boat.

A boat in the Fishermen's Museum. The museum provides a wealth of information on the history of fishing in the town.

The herring gull is the most common gull found in Hastings and is loved and loathed by the locals in equal measure.

The net huts were built tall to provide extra storage space.

Net huts along Rock-a-Nore Road.

Nets stored on the beach.

Mackerel can be caught in the summer off the harbour arm.

This boat is at the other end of town at Bulverhythe but still bears the RX registration.

This boat is on display along Rock-a-Nore Road.

Fishing tackle on the Stade beach.

The Stade fishing area in winter.

The boats come in a variety of sizes and colours.

Constant pounding by the sea has resulted in the harbour arm being rebuilt several times over the years. The old structure can be seen in the bottom right of the picture.

A boat being launched into the sea by tractor. The town has the largest beach-launched fishing fleet in Europe.

A boat in the harbour.

The RX registration means the boat is part of the Rye Bay Fishing fleet.

A traditional-style fishing boat and nets.

A tourist enjoying fresh local seafood at one of the many fish shops on the Stade.

Hastings miniature railway runs through the Stade.

EAST HILL LIFT

Behind the Stade is the East Hill Lift, or funicular railway, which ferries people to the top of the East Hill and the beginning of Hastings Country Park. It was designed by P.H. Palmer, a borough engineer, and opened in 1902. It was originally operated by a water ballast system and each car had a 600-gallon tank. The ballast system was replaced by an electric motor in 1974 and the original mahogany-framed cars were replaced in 1976. Today the lift is the steepest of its kind in the country, with a gradient of 1 in 1.28 over a distance of 265ft. The upper station resembles a castle and is often mistaken as Hastings Castle by visitors. Unfortunately, the lift is currently closed for repair.

The East Hill Lift, the steepest funicular railway in the country. The lift ferries passengers from the Stade to the top of the East Hill.

FESTIVALS
THE SEAFOOD AND WINE FESTIVAL

The Seafood and Wine Festival is held every year in September on the Stade coach park. It attracts thousands of visitors who can enjoy wine from nearby vineyards and the best in local seafood. As well as food and drink, some of the best local acts can be seen.

Crowds gather to watch local fishermen demonstrate net repairing skills at the Seafood and Wine Festival.

The best in locally caught fresh fish.

THE JACK-IN-THE-GREEN FESTIVAL

The Jack-in-the-Green Festival is a traditional English pagan festival held every May. The festival is celebrated nationally and was revived in Hastings in 1983 and has been held ever since. Hastings hosts one of the largest Jack-in-the-Green festivals, attracting visitors from all over the world.

The central figure of the festival is the Jack-in-the-Green. Its origins can be traced back to the 16th century when people would make garlands of flowers and leaves for May Day then cover a person in them. Their creations became more elaborate as different work guilds competed with each other, and Jack-in-the-Green was born. May Day was also the annual holiday of chimney sweeps, who adopted the festival for themselves.

For locals the festival is often regarded as the highlight of the Hastings calendar, and many participate in the parade which winds its way through the Old Town and culminates at the castle.

The Jack-in-the-Green. The Jack is covered in foliage from head to toe.

A local man painted in the traditional green.

Crowds at Hastings Castle gather to watch performances as part of the Jack-in-the-Green Festival.

Crowds enjoying a pagan dance at the Chess Square.

Morris dancers parading down George Street during the Jack-in-the-Green Festival.

'Fair Maidens' on show in the castle grounds.

GUY FAWKES CELEBRATIONS

Another popular event is the Guy Fawkes celebrations. The town celebrates with a spectacular parade, culminating on the beach for the jaw-dropping firework display.

Preparations for a huge bonfire on the beach.

An example of how people dress for the parade through town.

Fireworks over the town during Guy Fawkes night.

ST LEONARDS FESTIVAL

The St Leonards Festival is held every year. Kings Road captures the carnival spirit, with parades, exotic food and a multitude of people. The party then continues as Warrior Square Gardens hosts popular bands and performers from all over the world.

Warrior Square Gardens opened in 1852 as a subscription garden. The colourful gardens host the St Leonards Festival.

A local Samba musician enjoying the St Leonards Festival.

Kings Road in carnival spirit for the St Leonards Festival.

PARKS AND GARDENS

Hastings has many public parks and gardens on offer. Alexandra Park is the largest and is listed as a park of special interest by English Heritage. It was opened in 1882 and was designed by Robert Marnock, a famous horticulturist.

The park covers an area of 109 acres and includes a woodland, boating lake, tennis courts, bandstand, war memorial, peace garden and playground. Anglers can spend time fishing in Harmers Pond or Buckshole Reservoir.

The biggest event in the park is Hastings Beer and Music Festival, held every summer. It attracts thousands of visitors and some famous bands have played at the festival.

The garden of remembrance in Alexandra Park.

The war memorial marks the entrance to the park.

ON LAND
BURMA NORTH AFRICA
GALLIPOLI
FRANCE   PALESTINE

The park's boating lake. Sculptor Rick Kirby's piece *Continuum* can be seen in the lake. It consists of interweaving figures forming an arc.

The peace garden gates in Alexandra Park, made by local artist Lee Dyer.

A sculpture in the peace gardens.

Footpaths wind their way through the 109-acre park.

Waterways connect the
lakes and ponds.

Harmers Pond is a popular fishing spot for anglers in the park.

Ponds can be found throughout the park.

The Coronation Wood at the north of the park is a local nature reserve.

The gill runs from the north of the park through dense woodland.

The Gill Stream flows over several waterfalls.

ST LEONARDS GARDENS

These gardens were designed by James Burton, co-creator of London's Regent's Park. Situated in the heart of St Leonards, between Maze Hill and Quarry Road, the gardens were originally for the residents of the surrounding Burton houses. The Hastings Cooperation acquired them in 1880 and they have been open to the public ever since.

Views out to sea, as well as of Burton's Victoria Hotel and Assembly Rooms, can be seen from the top of the gardens. The central feature is an oriental-style pond dotted with water lilies.

The gardens recently benefitted from a Heritage Lottery Fund grant.

The lily-covered pond in the centre of St Leonards Gardens.

The entrance to the gardens is accessed through Burton's South Lodge.

174

A view from the top of Burton's St Leonards Gardens.

SUMMERFIELDS WOODS

Summerfields Woods are a semi-natural woodland, situated just a few minutes walk from the town centre. The 7.3 hectares of meadows, freshwater streams, ponds and reedbeds have been proposed as a local nature reserve. An interesting structure in the woods is the mock-Roman baths with ornate grotto area. It was constructed in the 1830s by Wastel Brisco and utilised a natural spring emerging through the sandstone. The original structure contained arches either side of the grotto.

The mock-Roman baths were designed in the 1830s.

The Victorian-style
Summerfields Woods.

HASTINGS COUNTRY PARK

Hastings Country Park extends from the East Hill as far as the village of Fairlight. The three miles of coastline include 267 hectares of ancient woodland, a disused quarry, gorse and heath hills, abundant wildlife, a holiday park and a nudist beach. The area became a country park in 1971 and it continues to attract thousands of visitors every year. There are a number of marked trails throughout the park and one can walk from the East Hill to Fairlight and beyond.

The park is within the High Weald Area of Outstanding Natural Beauty and has been designated a Site of Special Scientific Interest due to its biodiversity and geology. Peregrines and warblers have been spotted nesting off the cliff face, while weasels and stoats inhabit the woodlands. One might be lucky enough to spot the extremely rare *Lixus algirus*, a large weevil, or *Micaria romana*, an ant-eating spider. During certain times of the year porpoises and bottlenose dolphins can be spotted offshore.

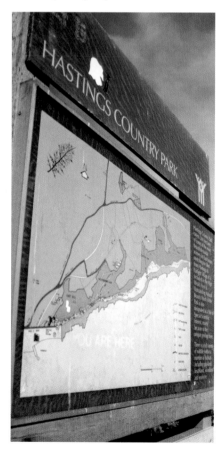

A map of Hastings Country Park, on top of the East Hill, marks the start of the park.

The beacon on top of the West Hill is lit every year during the bonfire celebrations – part of a series of beacons around the country.

The coastguard station on the cliff top at Fairlight overlooks the English Channel.

The low tide exposes the many rock pools and their wealth of wildlife.

Wild flowers on the cliff top of Ecclesbourne Glenn.

A trail winding its way through the valley of Ecclesbourne Glenn.

A trail leading through the country park towards Fairlight. The hillsides in the region are covered with gorse.

The trails lead through woodland as well.

The Firehills, part of the park.

The trails are signposted throughout the park.

Cattle grazing on the gorse–covered hills of Hastings Country Park.

The cliff top at Ecclesbourne Glenn, with the harbour arm in the background.

Local-style signposts along Barley Lane, which runs from Hastings to the country park.

The area is the habitat of many plant species.

Wild ponies grazing in Brakey Bank field. The Exmoor ponies were introduced to the park from nearby Irle, near Lewes. They help manage the area by controlling grasses and gorse.

Breathtaking views can be seen throughout the park.

This is where the East Hill meets Ecclesbourne Glenn.

Rock-a-Nore beach, where the high weald meets the sea. It is a popular bathing area.

The valley of Ecclesbourne Glenn at Hastings Country Park overlooks the English Channel. A variety of different tree species can be seen here, and ferns are one of the more common plants that can be found.

Filsham Reed Bed is the largest reed bed in the county, and it plays a
vital role in managing water flow through the valley.

FILSHAM REED BED

Filsham Reed Bed lies in West St Leonards, in the Bulverhythe area. It is the largest reed bed in the county and is part of the Coombe Haven wetland complex, a Site of Special Scientific Interest. It is home to several ecologically important species, including breeding bird populations, dragonflies, water beetles and plants.

The tranquil Filsham Reed Bed, which is managed by the Sussex Wildlife Trust.

Much of the area becomes flooded,
especially in the winter.

The Coombe Haven River runs directly through Filsham Reed Bed and provides a refuge for many species of bird.

Flora at Filsham Reed Bed.

The Pebsham area is surrounded by farmland, with rapeseed being a popular crop.

Crops being grown in surrounding fields.

During the summer months the area bursts into life.

A public footpath leading through woodland near the Filsham Reed Bed.

Bluebells cover the woodland
floor during the spring months.

Reeds dominate much of the area.

A public walkway through Filsham Reed Bed. Several species of rare bird, insect and plant can be found within its intricate waterways and marshes.

The unique freshwater ecology provides a haven for wildlife.

FAMOUS HASTONIANS
JOHN LOGIE BAIRD

John Logie Baird (1888-1946) was the inventor of the world's first television. He resided in Hastings in the 1920s and the town is sometimes referred to as the 'Birthplace of Television'. He gave his first demonstration of his system at number 21 Linton Crescent on 26 July 1923.

In 1924 Baird moved his workshop to number 8 Queens Arcade in the town centre. While there he accidentally electrocuted himself with 1,200 volts and was thrown across the floor. His landlord subsequently asked him to move out. With reluctance he left and moved to London to continue his work.

By 1924 news of his experiments had reached the national press and in 1926 he demonstrated his television to the Royal Institution. This led to Baird being granted a transmitting licence by the Post Office. His work attracted the interest of the BBC and in September 1929 they began a series of experimental television transmissions.

Baird's early television designs comprised a spinning cardboard disc cut from a hat box, a tin disc, some lenses from bicycle lights, wax, darning needles and a small electric fan motor. The first flickering images were of a Maltese cross, then later a ventriloquist's dummy and a human face. However, local physicist Victor Mills, who helped Baird, claims the first transmitted images were of his fingers.

Although Baird is credited with inventing the television his mechanical device was soon made obsolete by the invention of a truly electronic device by American inventor Philo Farnsworth in 1928.

Baird returned to Hastings in 1941 and lived in nearby Bexhill until his death in 1946.

A plaque outside John Logie Baird's residence at Queens Arcade, in the town centre.

Used with permission of Hastings Museum and Art Gallery.

Baird's television was a largely mechanical device consisting of spinning disks and strobing lights.

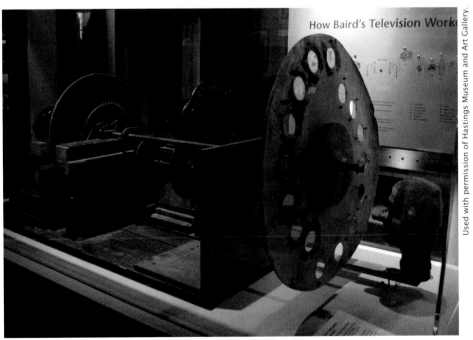

Used with permission of Hastings Museum and Art Gallery.

A dummy's head was used as an image in some of his early experiments.

GREY OWL

Grey Owl, or 'Wa-sha-quon-asin', meaning 'Great Horned One', was a Canadian writer and conservationist. Born in Hastings in 1888 with the name Archibald Belaney, the young Grey Owl grew up with his grandmother and aunts. He showed an interest in nature and native culture at a young age and worked briefly in a timber yard before he was sacked for throwing a bomb down his employer's chimney.

Used with permission of Hastings Museum and Art Gallery.

Native American artefacts on display at the Grey Owl exhibit.

Used with permission of Hastings Museum and Art Gallery.

Grey Owl as a child.

Used with permission of Hastings Museum and Art Gallery.

Woman Says "He's Belaney or I'll Eat My Hat"

"WHEN I first read his book and saw his portrait in the front of it—long before all this identity discussion arose—I said: 'Grey Owl is Archie Belaney or I'll eat my hat.'"

SPECIAL TO THE "EVENING ARGUS"

THE "Evening Argus" is able to reveal exclusively to-day that "Grey Owl," the famous "Indian" author and lecturer—known as the "Modern Hiawatha"—was a Hastings man.

Wa-Sha-Quon-Asin, as he called himself, was really Archibald Stansfeld Belaney, and his father was George Belaney, an architect.

November 24, 1937

GREY OWL, American Indian, naturalist and author, now in his second lecture tour of Britain, gave further sketches of life in the Canadian North-West when he lectured in the Lyric Theatre, Glas-

In these words, Mrs. D. M. Champness, of 88, Athelstan-road, Hastings, affirmed in an exclusive interview with an "Observer" reporter yesterday (Friday) her conviction that Grey Owl, the Red Indian author, lecturer and naturalist, was actually Hastings-born Archibald Stansfeld Belaney, a close friend of her family in his schooldays and nephew of the Misses A. and C. Belaney, who now live at 24, Wellington-road, Hastings.

AUNTS TELL STORY OF AMAZING WORLD HOAX

HAILED "MODERN HIAWATHA"

'Grey Owl,' In His Deerskin, Is Here As Envoy Of The Wild

By F. G. H. SALISBURY
SOUTHAMPTON, Thursday.

GREY OWL EXCITES AUDIENCE

Stirring Discourse at Winter Garden

Regrettably the name Grey Owl has been tarnished by revelation that he was not the Indian he claimed to be

"Once I was a hunter," he continued, "and the Beaver was my game. Then I married. Anaharco did not like this hunting business. The cruelty of it got under her skin."

Old Hastonian who became Red Indian

After Grey Owl's true identity was discovered, newspapers revealed his story.

In 1906 he emigrated to Canada and worked as a fur trapper. While there he met a woman from the Anishinaabe tribe and they married. It was at this time that he began to call himself 'Grey Owl', claiming he was the child of a Scottish father and Apache mother and had moved to Canada from the US.

While serving in World War One he was shot in the foot, which led to his discharge. He returned to Canada in 1917 and in 1925 met Gertrude Bernard, a Mohawk Iroquois woman. She encouraged him to stop trapping and to instead publish his writings about his life in the wilderness. He went on to release many books, articles and documentary films and also gave lectures.

In 1935 he began a tour of England, including Hastings, to educate people on conservation issues. However, the tour had a detrimental effect on his health and in 1938 he died of pneumonia.

Grey Owl.

Used with permission of Hastings Museum and Art Gallery.

Throughout his working life Archibald Belany always went under the name 'Grey Owl' and professed his Apache ancestry. It was not until after his death that his true identity became known, which resulted in his books ceasing to be published. The newspapers exposed his true identity with sensational front-page headlines and public interest in conservation began to decline.

It was not until many years after his death that the importance of Grey Owl's teachings became apparent. Today, Grey Owl is remembered through his various writings and films. In Hastings Country Park there is a commemorative plaque and at Hastings Museum and Art Gallery there is an exhibition of his life.

ELIZABETH BLACKWELL

Elizabeth Blackwell was the first woman to qualify as a doctor in 1849 and the first to be placed on the British Medical Register in 1859. She graduated from New York's Geneva College but found it difficult to get work in the American hospitals so she moved to Paris. While there she contracted an eye infection from a baby she was treating, which resulted in it being replaced with a glass one.

In 1857, along with her sister Emily, she founded the New York Infirmary for Indigent Women and Children. She trained many women during the American Civil War and after it ended she established the Women's Medical College.

She returned to England in 1869 and taught at the London School of Medicine for Women. A year later she retired, but still continued to write lectures on the Women's Rights Movement and the importance of education.

She died of a stroke in her Hastings home on 31 May 1910.

A plaque commemorating Elizabeth Blackwell. It reads, 'One who never turned her back but marched breast forward. Never doubted clouds would break. Never dreamed, though right were worsted, wrong would triumph. Held we fall to rise, are baffled to fight better, sleep to wake.'

The house of Elizabeth Blackwell. It is situated at the foot of the East Hill, overlooking the Old Town.

SIDNEY LITTLE

Sidney Little, known along the south coast as the 'concrete king', was an influential borough engineer. In the 1930s Little transported the town from the Victorian age to the 20th century with his abundant use of concrete.

One of his best-known creations was Bottle Alley, an underpass along the seafront from the pier to Warrior Square. Little found a quantity of broken bottles on a rubbish tip and set them into the concrete walls, creating a striking pattern along the underpass.

Little's largest project was the bathing pool in West St Leonards.

A view from Bottle Alley towards the South Downs. Beachy Head, the highest cliff in the country, can be seen meeting the sea.

The upper promenade of Bottle Alley.

Sidney Little's Bottle Alley. The alley is decorated with broken bottles set in concrete.

These shelters are one of the few remaining examples of Little's work.

These beach huts in West St Leonards stand
on the same spot as Little's bathing pool
complex once did.

MODS AND ROCKERS

During the summer of 1964 Hastings witnessed clashes between the mods and the rockers. The troubles started in Brighton and spilled over into Hastings, culminating on the August Bank Holiday. The newspapers at the time described the clashes as being of 'disastrous proportions', and labelled the participants 'vermin' and 'louts'.

Today, there is still a vibrant subculture of mods and rockers in the town, but they are more likely to be found playing music together than fighting.

Used with permission of Hastings Museum and Art Gallery.

An authentic Hastings mod scooter at the Hastings Museum.

A mod versus rocker exhibit at the Hastings Museum and Art Gallery.

Used with permission of Hastings Museum and Art Gallery.

The town still proves popular with mods.